SPIRIT

COPYRIGHT PAGE

TABLE OF CONTENTS

TABLE OF CONTENTS

DEDICATION

INVITATION

CELEBRATIONS

Out of Mud	12
Riverbed Erosion	13
Morning	14
Sunflower	16
A Seasonal Spring Poem	18
A Walk Along Upper Big Bluestem	21
No Great Hunger	22
This Afternoon	25
Lessons from Nature	26
Luna Llena	27
Moon	28
Moongifts	30
Stars in Twigs	31

RELATIONS

The Gift of a Grandmother	34
Kin	35
A Poem for the Youth	37
A Love Poem to the World	39
My Mother	40

Because of You…	41
Because of You	44
Prodigal Son	45
Refuge	46
Heartbreak	47

INVOCATIONS

Becoming	50
Changing…	51
Faith	52
Calling on the Benevolent	53
Build Worlds with Me	54
Just Enough	55
I Will	55
Poem your Thoughts	56
Creation	59
The Color of My Skin	60
Is Not a Question	60
World-Gazing	72
For All to See	75
Sight	77
Looking Around	79
Seen	81
Peace	82
Light	82

HOMECOMINGS

From Every Child   84

Evolutionary   89

Before   92

Unspeakable You   94

Allowance of Being   95

Rainbow Bridges   97

I Wonder   99

Curiosity   101

Love Shine   102

Journey into Self   107

Return Trip: 109

A Lesson on the Labyrinth   109

BEGINNINGS

A Miracle   112

Miracle   113

Market Correction   114

Currency   114

God's Gallery   115

Creating Reality   117

With Words   117

What Now?   118

New Beginnings   120

Radicle - Ode to 12/21/2020   121

BOOK MATTER

LANDING SPIRIT   124

GRATITUDES   131

DEDICATION

....

For You, Dear One

INVITATION

Welcome to the weaving of words threaded by two poets who found kinship in their expressions of SPIRIT. May you enjoy the dance of poetry as you braid yourself into their alternating poems, dancing alongside the words in celebration! Should you be curious about the story of how SPIRIT landed and the relationship the authors developed, you will find the telling at the end of the book. And now, let us begin...

CELEBRATIONS

....

OUT OF MUD

Out of mud
a lotus
blooms

Now,
a butterfly
fully in plume

Next,
it may
be a star
far off in the sky

And then, who knows ...

Perhaps a God -
upon whom people
ask why

RIVERBED EROSION

Soft lumber
peregrinator
transcribing benthos to air
loosening memory from pebble
whisper of knowledge released
straight to starlight

MORNING

The starlings have come this morning
though usually arriving in afternoons

Their chirps are soothing
alerting
the cat of silver
keeping tabs
steady tail wags
Pulls back curtains
more than a sliver
Streaming in light
where in bed
I would rather
lay
so begins my day.

Soon upon the feeders
in turn by size
First the tiny
finches
sparrows
the chickadee
a nuthatch
woodpecker, occasionally

Then follow the mediums -
cardinals, a loud blue jay
robins, if its spring

starlings come again
grackles with long tails
blue florescent chest

the mourning doves
take their time

a new bird appeared
one day!
red-breasted grosbeak

When cloudy
one might see
a hawk: coopers or red-tailed
little birds make easy prey

The squirrels they are not
phased by blocks
on feeders keeping them from feed
knock them over
to get to the shiny morsel
of sunflower seed

SUNFLOWER

One...
Pre-dawn
    Swollen green morsels
speak whispers
    of light
Energy of eventual
    bursting, gathering
rays up inside
    Magic soup
Leaves tender and new

Two...
Her galaxy begins
    to traipse
through time, one
    pioneering petal...
More...spiral opening
    Attracting the powers
that be
    Beetle kin drinking
Dew drops

Three...
Radiance, oh radiant
        Oh, radiate
Beams of light my
        Heart obeys
Soul-flower-cosmic-speak
        Your sex mirrors the spiral
Of your petals
        Centering, centering
To center
        the bees answer

Four...
Matronly deepening relationship
        Erotic now speaks infinity
Consumed into a multiplicit world
        now Goldfinch befriends you
Your death is as glorious
        As your birth
Light shining
        Eternal mirth

A SEASONAL SPRING POEM

Crabapples, apple blossoms, cherry
Daffodils, hyacinths, tulips -
Variety aplenty.

Spring's wondrous gifts
awakening the coolest of hearts
Scents, colors and *green*

Longer days, warmer breezes
Profusion of color
in sweet succession

Some say they bloom
too short
But yet they *do* bloom

Those same tire of the flower
when black-eyed susans
bloom the whole of summer

Can you imagine…
to tire
 of a flower?
God's most precious jewels?

One day, it is cool
the redbuds spring open
Like tiny lips proclaiming joy

Now magnolias and dogwoods, too
join in with exuberance
Just when you think
spring has shed its innocent splendor

Columbine soon will be in line
Like God, as if to say,
I'm still here,
gaze upon My hues,
stay in Love.

The next day may be hot
Reminding us of summer's turn
Pastels still light our path

The grass stretches up and out
The rains and winds
blow petals all about

Begging for shade will wait
for now
we walk in comfort
soft loose clothes

Lilacs' sweet perfume seeps into my being
I feel young again
Renewed, refreshed, alive

Only now can I recognize
the depth of slumber winter
put me in.

I am awake now –
How could I have fallen
so deep, asleep,
yet carried on my daily way?

Summer brings another
kind of slumber
slow, lazy, relaxed

Until, again, Autumn arrives
to remind us of our
needed winter preps

Rich bodied
colors changing
Fruits ripening, leaves falling,
until the garden rests.
Rains, winds then snows
temperatures fall,
short days,
long night tucked away

And slowly, we drift away again
In rehearsed ways
Into the cold and dark once more.

The faint memory of renewal
guiding each sleepy step
waiting for
that moment
we will feel alive again

The sweet taste of fruits
reminding us of the seeds
which we will plant

The flowers, berries
bees, butterflies and birds
the buzz, flutter and song

How these cycles
keep me turning
towards the season for
which I long:
Aaaaah - Spring!

A WALK ALONG UPPER BIG BLUESTEM

Trickle, swell, roll, and bloom
Bird song dripping from tree to tree
Enraptured folds of swaying green
Heart string sings in tune

Butterflies on nectar swoon
Lily! Aster! Queens of the bee
Immersed in your colorful glee
Dancing in sacred womb

Musk of pine, herb, and rose
Spreading in warmth, swirling in air
Brilliance of colors, my soul laid bare

Lying within your throes
Becoming sound, sky, scent, and ground
Right here, in this moment, forever found

NO GREAT HUNGER

No great hunger
stirs in my belly.

No great ache
has its hold on my heart
(any longer.)

No great curiosity
swirls in my mind.

No great lust
longs in my loins.

No great thirst
has me salivating.

Yet, I am still very much
Alive!

My days pass like moods
filling base needs
of food, warmth, caring
for the nest and brood.

Yet, each is driven beyond survival - A Purpose.

A purpose which asks of us patience,
waiting until such time as we are called.

And in the waiting -
in the patience, lies a paradox.

The great need to be of service and
the great reluctance to be called at all.

For to feel truly fulfilled,
one must spend oneself completely.

But to spend oneself completely,
one must already know the feeling of fulfillment.

No great sadness -
the illusions of the mind

So, what *is* pregnant in me?

The great beauty and design
of the Master's Universe.

The GRANDNESS and
the minuscule . . .

what
captivates me is
an intense fascination
of creation - the earth, her
greenery, blues and depths of
the ocean, the sun, sky, bright and
starry, farthest reach of our galaxy,
of all kinds and types and shapes
the sheer number of all things,
the cycles, and the seasons,
slight differences in the
variety, subtle shades
in the color of
a grape.

THIS AFTERNOON

Hand to mallet to drum
Frogs sing
Soil softens
Moon hides
Clouds think alive
Tree opens
Runner swiftly smiles
Creek overflows
Clovers open
Feet press down
Air swallows mosquitoes
Sun dips
Mountain watches
Young deer forages
Song reverberates within

LESSONS FROM NATURE

Bloom where you are planted,
so a saying goes.
No feet, nor wings has a blossoming rose.

Bears have feet like us
and like them, sometimes we need to
hibernate.

Birds have wings,
and instincts and thermal winds.

From them, we can learn
that sometimes, we too, may choose
to migrate.

LUNA LLENA

Gulping glorious flow
Swallow exhale reverent
Present heart the covenant

Laughing wildly
Silver bright and shadowy
Full and magnificent
Alive and relevant

She in full glory
Telling all stories
Llena de color
A ella todo honor

Celebración!
Ahora, we have come

MOON

Ask not the full wax moon
to dim her light

Nor the waning moon
to shine bright

For each in turn
shall have its purpose

And just in time
will surely surface

Trust, Trust, Trust

Ask not for any than the more
Nor shall ye dim yours

All you have,
is all you have to live

In the push and the pull
sometimes you take, sometimes you give

Allow, Allow, Allow

Cycles of time
rhythm and rhyme
all in turn, all in time

Who is to say which is which
in the wax and the wane?

The Moon - she waxes and she wanes,
and though you may not see her,
isn't she there
just the same?

MOONGIFTS

She offers her sweet crescent glow
Existing among vast eternal night
Held within light points untold
She beckons forth bloom of internal Sight

Embrace her arched concavity
Arise to invisible Truth
In heart you'll find her gravity
Across the sky, vow turned loose!

STARS IN TWIGS

I walk toward her at night
Feel the clinging molecules of dry humidity
upon grass and skin,
Smell crisp winter air
breaking in my lungs

And there:
She stands in recognition.
Her silhouette a mirror -
entryway,
Cottonwood,
Grandma.
Pulling me closer
as her instincts do.

Listen like the full moon
hears the sun at night.
Hear her silence,
punctuated by vole and breath.

Feel as pebble feels,
rounded by creek.
Feel magnitude.

Feel convergence
Feel convection
Feel converted

Feel as she feels.

The souls of my feet
walk the outline of her moon shadow,
I am touching myself.
Touch,
as she touches condensed moonlight.
I walk into her musk
and disappear.

RELATIONS

....

THE GIFT OF A GRANDMOTHER

I only watched her from afar
To her, I was a distant memory

After having 11 children, add their spouses,
her first grandchild aligned with her own last infant,
arriving quicker than she could count.
But count she could,
even without a formal education.

I longed to sit by her
well worn feet and
hear her stories of old.
Share her secrets only
reserved for the Truth-teller,
she frequently visited.

This treasured gift of a grandmother
I longed for was in time
given to my only son.
This desire took a generation to be honored.
Its gift can only arrive in the future.

KIN

Sometimes
a hand is held out to you
In the quiet, unfurled spaces
Like along a path of oak leaves
orange-gold lit from inside, muted and pungent
each step soothing your thoughts
into their original resting position

In this moment
we met.
She, past fawn, not yet doe
Me, past remembering, not yet forgotten
kneeled before her

Funny how these encounters open time
like unfolding a fresh blanket
to make room for another,
the Outstretched Hand,
to lay beside you

We touched upon the breeze
her flaring nostrils composing me,
legs slightly splayed below the knees,
white patch on her throat.

And she walked towards me:
towards the call of Kin,
the Outstretched Hand weaving two threads
back into the cloth that enfolds them

How deep can we feel our kinships?

She daintily continued about her day
up the slope
I put one foot in front of the other
beginning my walk again

A POEM FOR THE YOUTH

Remember some of the old,
When you bring in the new.

Things which worked,
The tried and the true.

Lessons learned
from years of trials.

Errors made,
practices in piles.

Build upon
a foundation of the past.

It is what
allowed us to move this fast.

The pace of today
built on slower roads of yesterday.

Branch out,
Innovate; the past, respect pay.

Soon your new
will be their old.

You'll thank them
for valuing your hard won gold.

Each generation
builds upon the past.

Layer by layer,
legacy is cast.

Higher and higher,
we climb.

Reaching for
that next level of sublime.

A LOVE POEM TO THE WORLD

It doesn't matter if we can't go back
to sand away the coarse grains of our damage
I want to know the texture
of your heart-wood
I want to know if the capillaries are
pulling up fresh sap
As if anything in this world is symmetrical, anyhow
Allow the motley bark to hold the tender places close
When the great fire comes burning
through the forest of our stories
I will find you cracked
fortified
With a path cleared for your searching roots

MY MOTHER

My
light,
My love
My union
My ecstasy
The embrace
of our Hearts
My Mother
my soul.

To face her
I need the greatest light
to meet her where she is -
to see her clearly,
her warm
compassionate heart,
her ever-loving
giving self.

BECAUSE OF YOU...

Because of beautiful you,
I exist.

Because there is beautiful me,
I have a handsome son.

Because I want him to know
all the gifts I treasure,
I look to you.

Because you have always fed me
I have never known hunger.

Because you kept me covered in the cold,
I have known only warmth.

Because of your constant concerns
for my well-being,
I have always felt protected.

Because you have sacrificed much
and had to do without often,
I take nothing for granted.

Through your caring and
kindness towards others,
You taught me compassion.

Because you labored to create
artistic gourmet food,
I have learned to savor every bite.

Because of your careful tending
of gardens,
I look for life lessons in nature.

Because of your dedication and
belief in God,
I know to daily nurture my soul.

Because of your strong sense of community,
I have a strong foundation.

By gracefully coping with all of
life's inevitable surprises,
You taught me to accept change as part of life's journey.

Because of all these gifts and more,
I know that I am deeply loved.

If I am able to pass along just half of these gifts to my son,
I will know that I, too, am a good mother.

Words alone (in any language) cannot begin to express
all of the appreciation that I feel.

For all the treasured values you have shared,
I am eternally grateful.

Happy Mother's Day
I love you.
Today and everyday.

BECAUSE OF YOU

Because of your resilience
   I learned positivity is a choice
Because of your compassion
   I know my own worth
Because of your sincerity
   I learned to lead with my heart
Because you value well-being
   I learned to care for my body
Because you love unconditionally
   I found joy inside myself

The tender act of rubbing my back
as a child at bedtime
Gifted me with knowing
I belong to this world

I grow strong because of the rich soil you nurture
Every day, each moment

Because of your grace
   I am filled with gratitude

PRODIGAL SON

Man gifted with so many seeds
So many competing
For her egg limiting
Woman knows how precious each one is

The one who makes it through
On pedestal she grows
Takes her time to name
Name determines destiny
Reminds of why one came
A peaceable victory

REFUGE

Come, it is time
Believe in the safety of my gentle appreciation
Walk into the tender sore spaces you call suffering
Your body knows the way

You don't need your banner
Or to make an announcement
Or to check the time
It is time to be known
It is time to ratify yourself

Meanwhile, allow your ugly, glorious unfurling
To fall into my terrifying, divine reception
Together we are all that and more
Together we are none of this
All the time
Side by side
We'll hold hands
The whole way Home

HEARTBREAK

I can only bow until I am prostrate
My heart is ripped open by your words
I release the sap of my entrenched ache
Into sacred ground where I am heard
Finding roots, outreaching in loving uptake
Capillaries giving home to all left unsaid
Allowing for leaves to flourish exponential
From this spilling of Love so red

INVOCATIONS

....

BECOMING

Read this bottom to top, right to left.

becoming constant your alongside Self inhabit to platforms
body your are words these
creation and jubilation vibrant of act an in
them upon pull you event the in

intact

return your for here lie words these
conception narrow
their hold to big too place a
into propulsion for fuel

irrelevant

them renders that truth reveal to only existing words

meaning their know you until away drop to letters the allow
yourself for words these inside feel
sound for words these between listen

CHANGING...

New times
Call for new paradigms

One generation
Shares its reality

The next seeks
To create more certainty

An ancient strand,
A wisp of fresh born air

Essential truths
Are timeless in essence

Preservers
of these laws are well aware

Newer truths
Emerge from Adolescence

Ethereal thread,
Root primordial

Two threads
To be woven in careful braid

Each the keeper of wisdom
Luminous

The natural laws growing
Entwined, obeyed

Toward light most high
- Nirvana of Us

FAITH

My capacity reflects
my infinitude:
Gentle power raw and
chaotic and inviting
once it
lands in you.
Atop my throne, the key a
simple word from
the Blue:

Nothing can hurt me.
Death is not absolute.

Lightening, thunder and
delectable rain
sexing the land. I ran from it
until I ran into it.

Protection and safety are helpful proxies,
while I'm in my stupor fleeing from nothing.
Meanwhile,
the world
explodes in ecstasy.

CALLING ON THE BENEVOLENT

The altruistic
The visionaries
The optimistic
The ones who truly care
Step up and take your post
In leadership
We've gone too far astray

Take the helm
And captain this ship
The deck we'll have to clean
Yesterday's muck
And when it's spic and span
Well make the plan
To return to healthy prosperity

Those who made the mess
Will have to face
The soap and sponge
The broom and the mop
Lessons forgotten along the way

Those who suffered shall
Have their recompense
apologies and justice

Let's move together
To rebuild for all
Poised and prepared
A better day and way

BUILD WORLDS WITH ME

I am unafraid
   of exposure;
   direct line of sight
I speak into my scars
   -shiny and smooth-
   the secret of their
   unravelling
Ownership is mine:
   I claim my work
   and occupy my emotions
I am my own reference point:
   self-begotten,
   self-generating
Agency is unapologetic:
   I am not victim
   I am transformer
I am not sorry for needing something:
   I can show up to you
   Can you show up to me?
I tune my frequency to love:
   I want to harmonize
   Let us amplify

All this really means is:
I have the courage to stay.
I have the courage to leave.

Build worlds with me.

JUST ENOUGH

"The poor" are neither ignorant nor ever accustomed to their poverty
If everyone took just enough
Instead of reserve for just a handful few
Then each and all could have and live in opulence
If we allowed that which was renewable to renew

The Source from which it comes, continuous and everlasting
For this world's bounty is plenty and great
Free will is our right in determining how bright it will illuminate.
I wonder, each moment when given the choice, make which, will we?

Too much, too little, or just enough?

Will I?

Will you?

I WILL

Singing up to the stars
Yes, I will fulfill my agreement
Wailing down to the ground
Yes, I will fulfill my agreement

I lay upon you
Spherical nourishment seeping in
light spilling
goddess willing

I vow the softness of a Cottonwood seed
the silence of a sun baked desert rock
and the fervor of a dawn chorus in July

Yes,
I will fulfill my agreement

POEM YOUR THOUGHTS

Oh, your thoughts…

Your fearful thoughts
Where were they bought?

From your mother or preacher
Or your second grade teacher

Television programming
With news ever alarming

Your dad who yelled
The man that smelled

To whom did you turn the purse over
To wish upon the four leaf clover

Protect your self from the evil eye
And all bad things which could make you die

Your thoughts, my friend, belong to you
Just like your pants and that sweet hairdo

With cash in hand you made a trade
Trust and faith is what you paid

At first they tingle and excite
But then you felt their painful bite

Once you tire of fights, fire and hate
It's up to you to pick a better fate

You can leave behind the suffering and strife
With words you create your reality, your life

As way leads to way
One great Buddha did say

When you have tired of stress-filled fear
Allow these words to gently steer

It's as easy as choosing your prose for who knows,
perhaps it would not have smelled as sweet
Were it not called a rose

Born of love, innocence pure
Return to these for the cure

Empty your mind of harmful words
Float them free like carefree birds

Then fill the now cleared space
With words that bless and grace

Words that raise your spirit high
Stretch your arms towards the sky

Make a list, words that attract
Who you are, not how you act

Agapé, serendipity
These words make me happy

Raise your frequency to high vibrate
Attract your destiny's soulmate

The power of Love, the sweetness of joy
The thrill of Peace for all to enjoy

Beauty, flowers all abound
Which fun words have you found

Now note the shift in tone
Beginning to now, in this poem

Follow your feelings as we rose
The energy in the words we chose

Like angel wings in art
Softly opening the heart

Give yourself this gift each day
Choosing words to think and say

Paving a path of light
Which serves to lift and delight

Simply by adding your glee
To this earth, a blessing be

Natural is your state of calm
Love is the natural balm

CREATION

We are all wombs
Wombs beget words
Words are all webs
Webs are wonderings
Wonderings are wakefulness
Wakefulness is World
World is We

THE COLOR OF MY SKIN
IS NOT A QUESTION

Are you black or are you white?
Young eyes for answers stared at me,
at first this question's bite

Even at the tender age of eight,
reserved and oh so shy,
I did not want to take that bait

the color of my skin is not a choice
and so,
the color of my skin is not a question
it just is

Never had I met a person
to whom I could assign,
these non-skin tones to
to describe a rainbow's range

where i come from, I see
a sea of humanity

of cultures, creeds, languages,
foods, heritage and geography

sizes, shapes of face
dialects, distinctions of place

For I am neither black
nor white
as they classify

It raises another query:
What exactly
are they asking of me?

Country of my birth or of my ancestors,
culture, religion or ethnicity?

My color is a shade
of brown, I suppose
which I have yet to define

Mocha, carmel, latte
honey or chai tea?
So many shades to chose from
and a spectrum in between.

The country of my origin
of my ancestors may mostly be
India

As such
Their religion may have been many
Sikh, Zoroastrian, Buddhist,
or most likely,
Hinduism

That is, until in no order and repeating,
the crusaders and British
came to conquer territory,
and converted some to
Christianity

When the Muslims came
they too, expanded followers to
Islam

The Mongols rode in
bringing with them
devastation and ingenuity -
what remains is a blend

You see, there is no clear border,
no boundary, no end
to the variety of colors of skin.

In proclaiming that I was Indian,
they began singing war chants.
Here, there was only one way to be Indian,
a long history of Native Americans.
Could such a vast continent have held only red skins?

To clarify further, I began calling myself Asian.
Could such a vast continent define my skin?
Then, they couldn't understand
why my eyes weren't slanted.

It gets interesting still
for my place of birth
is Africa

In this,
I am African,
not black

I assimilated
in a town of caucasians
where I became American,
not white

What kind of choice is this?
My skin is not a choice, it is unique
my skin is my gift, my individuality

Then came the forms
in mandatory census
asking questions
which felt like a life sentence
of a made up thing called race-
listed in a pre-supposed descending order.

What are you? Please check the box:
☐ Caucasian,
☐ African,
☐ or other

Of course,
I checked the "other",
convincing myself
that it stood for
the *human* race.

Can you imagine, walking around
with your identity
as an indescript
"other?"
In time, more boxes were added,
Excited to see the added exposure to diversity,
I searched eagerly for my personal identity:

☐

Asian/Pacific/Eastern Islander
    (*they* are all the same, right?)
☐ Mexican/Spanish/Hispanic
    (*them*, too?)
☐ Vietnamese/Korean
    (and again?)
☐ Somalian/Ethiopian
    (because of geography?)

Of what benefit was this and to whom?
At least, we were learning
there were other countries and continents!

And when in prejudice and fear
habits passed to them
by their parents and their peers,
strangers on streets exclaimed,
  "Go back to where you came from!",
I stood in silence stunned.

Where would that exactly be?
For years, it went.
My confusion may now be clear - Can you see?
When I, in college, now much less shy,
shared with friends
of the prejudice I'd faced,
their response made me smile,

"You're more American
than apple pie!"

So, if the color of my skin is not a question
what we are ignoring is the bigger deal

What questions we are being asked
versus what *we* should be asking

Politicians dream up
divisions to
polarize,
differentiate,
separate, segregate,
marginalize,

Pushing to extremes
Parting the Red Sea

We are asked,
Are you left or are you right?
Still not answering at thirty-eight

For I walk the full
line on every continuum,
making choices from
where I stand

and that could change
in a moment, day or year
from new demands
of mood and circumstance

Like most I think -
and because I do -
my choices vary
and most often
land in the middle
of the query

Neither, or both, or somewhere in-between

Are you black or are you white?
Independent, progressive
socialist, communist, democracy
liberal, conservative, revolutionary
Labels are labels
they stick

with bias as their glue
Once stuck,
they
get
i c k y

Solidarity, is in unity
Here's the irony
the same principle
In nationalism
Is what is great in Oneness

Power in some hands
is destructive
And in others, creative

There are greater issues
at stake for the sake of all our futures
When we focus only on the personal
we risk the long view and
what is good for all in the long run

These things are decidedly personal,
which is why "the They" choose them
to get your goat and make you take a stand
In these, each should choose for self only:
healthcare, abortion, gay marriage, immigration,
vaccines, racism and gun control, etc.
- opinions too many - we will never all agree
Where's the black or white in that?
In these, all our skins are too thin
by design
of individuality

This game of smoke and mirrors
while we are crazed to look at the left hand
ask "what is the right doing?"

No longer have we
time to squander
on debates and
on the gerrymander

There are things on which we can agree
Things like corporate Greed
and general disharmony
Corporations are made of people,
some climbed the apple tree
lured by sins, all seven, deadly

Can we recount them?
three by three?
Let's make a list:

Greed, we said,
And the other six?
Sloth, Lust, and Envy
Pride, Wrath, Gluttony

If the color of my skin is not a question
What should we be asking?
So many questions beyond the basic.

What really matters?
What is our purpose?
What shall we do with this momentary
 spark
- this gift of life -
this heaven on earth
to be remembered for all of eternity?

My opinion, as is my hope
for the many, always resides
in what is good for the whole
and balanced for the *every* me

To make room for
race, creed, genus, species,
Animalia, genes,
kinds, types, shapes, size
dimensions, layers,
We need just to make the circle bigger

On this planet, we are One
She needs us, and we need Her,
More

What is good for Her survival
keeps us *_alive_*

Even if we found other planets
to inhabit,
does it make sense to pillage her,
our only home, to risk it?

How many billions of years
did it take to arrive
at this level of evolution,
superiority and ignorance
this beauty

Do we really think we can replace it
in less than another eternity?

Are _you_ black or are _you_ white?
Let us ask this
in her current plight,
of our dear

Mother
Earth.

WORLD-GAZING

Do you remember the moment you first looked around?
Fluttering eyelids still adjusting,
contemplating entrance into a world
dense and viscous
You, still leaping in and out of pulses
as if choosing which fruit to eat by testing this fragrance,
and then another.

Flickers of intrigue invited your focus outward
and your eyes gazed softly, at first,
towards
contrast and purpose:

rough, smooth
bright, dull
round, sharp
vast, minute.
Encapsulated images
holding still for your searching stare

And you ate the fruit.
And your eyes built a world.
Wide-eyed and freely receiving,
you saw
A world in which you knew companionship
A world in which you learned the spectrum of gestures
Do you remember?
Wild witnessing of creation, over and over…

And do you remember what else you were looking at?
Your other eye,
turned toward your Origin?
It was unflinching.
Silently streaming Self unto yourself
Feeding you the essences of the fruits
so you could see your creation clearly
Whether or not you knew of this inward gaze
was unimportant.

Until the day you noticed an Eagle
tracing your periphery,
circling the edges of your knowing,
under a sky that folded
itself in on you
Your outward eyes utterly unfamiliar with
this long-forgotten gyroscope
of directionless light points

And remember, then,
you sank down to the bottom of the well?
And waited in the dark.
Breathless,
for long stretches of imagination,
until finally,
the acceleration of your world within Worlds
lifted you…

And at long last,
you found You.
Your center within Center.
All eyes focused,
glinting with wild laughter.

And now, your Blinking Eyes,
your Unflinching Eye,
complete you.
You have claimed your Vision.
Beheld by all eyes,
ripe,
brimming with nectar,
seen,
unseeable,
lit from within.

FOR ALL TO SEE

The full-ish moon
exposed my foolish dreams
for all to see.

What grand theatre
Did I threaten to grace
for all to see?

Which message loomed largest
Woven inside our tapestry
for all to see

Which is solution
and which is the question
for all to see.

Within the ordinary
Lies the *extra*-ordinary
for all to see.

I was already incredible
before I sought to be credible
for all to see.

Your gifts, too, shine within
awaiting their turn
for all to see.

The All is One
One is All there is
for all to see.

SIGHT

The eye keeps opening.
Wings spread,
my throat a dam holding the
surge
of Clarity's gush:

SPEAK!

-mind is flooded-
responding to stimuli, pulsing
with emergent urgency.
Relief appears, outlined, amidst the camouflage...

...clarity dissolves camouflage...
Bells! Whistles! Flags!

And you must see.
You have to see.
There is only seeing.
Horrific exposure,
pristine possibility:
you are called to swell through
your Vision.

A cataract does not shy away from the precipice.

This world is built in relief:
Topographic emotions
Cycling psyches
Flooding hearts
Deserted beliefs

We are the blueprint our Vision reveals!

LOOKING AROUND

When I look around,
I see so much beauty in every moment.

I am over-filled with the softness of a blanket,
the touch of paper, its grains and textures; the colors of ink,
of rainbows, of flowers, of everything.

The feel of wood and stone, the space and smell of trees,
the sight and flight and sound of birds, of the sheer variety.

The scent of fresh air. Moments of breathlessness. Breath
itself.

This is LIFE - the most beautiful, colorful thing our Creator
could imagine and has made.

And in it, He chose us! to behold his own creation and to
hold and co-create alongside Spirit.

Source wants us to know this truth, so we can be more
effective in our quest of "better."

The reason we always strive for "better" - it is an
evolutionary urge built-in.

It's all good. In the beginning. In the end. And again. The cycle spirals up.

Gratitude for God being.

SEEN

The world is awake to us
We may choose any moment to unwrap
The silk scarf blanketing our mind
Buffering the winds
Of sagittal motion.
Pause and de-robe,
My love…
Become available to the World's sight -
Complete the circuit

The World knows your gratitude
As milk-honey
Rising like sap through your limbs,
Nourishing the Great Being.
Gift yourself to the endless river,
My love…
Give yourself to the current
Of our lustrous mystery

PEACE

There have been
many
wars,

There is
only
One
Peace.

LIGHT

Cosmic
Enzymes
Condense
Intent
Palpable
Waves
Emerge
Singing
Alive

HOMECOMINGS

FROM EVERY CHILD

When you are happy -
I am happy.

When you tell me of the dangers of the world -
I am filled with fear for you and for me
and know the need for protection.

When you tell me of a Greater Being
who cares and looks out for us -
I am filled with safety, security
and know that we are protected.

When you are safe, I am safe.

When you tell me of all the grief and heartache
in the world -
I am filled with sadness and want to go
and hide.

When you tell me that all the suffering
is short-lived and has lessons to offer
when we quiet our mind -
I listen for the lesson
and open up to the world's pain
to seek the deeper joy.

When you tell me the wrongdoings
you feel others have done to you,
I am filled with hate and anger
and feel separated from others.

When you tell me that all make mistakes,
and that all mistakes are born of a disconnection
from love -
I am filled with empathy and want to return others home
to Love.

When you tell me that others are watching
and thinking about me and that
my actions and behaviors should live up to their
expectations -
I am filled with the anxiety of the possibility of making a
mistake.
I try either too hard, not enough, or not at all - to avoid
this perceived calamity.

When you tell me that you and God
are always watching over me and thinking of me,
that the good I do -
I do only for God, for you, for others, for me;
then I believe in myself and just do good.

When you act like daily life is a struggle,
I feel tired and helpless and powerless.

When you take charge of a bad situation,
and do what is in your power to make it good,
no matter the outcome -
I feel empowered and strong
and helpful.

When you walk through life carrying only
the critical view that others
have shared with you of yourself -
I feel a great burden and sadness;
I feel ugly, worthless and unlovable.

When you tell me that God gives us each unique gifts,
and that the best gift of all is LIFE,
I am filled with gratitude and I cherish who God made me.
I am filled with LOVE.

When you are happy,
I feel LOVED!

When I hear you complain of things
we have no control over -
I am filled with the futile desire
to solve problems bigger than my ability
and I feel small.

When you take positive control of things
within your realm and within your reach -
I feel capable and recharged!

When you cherish yourself -
I cherish myself.

When you express joy -
I feel joyful.

When you express wonder -
I want to learn more.

When you walk with a spring in your step,
I feel light enough to fly.

When you really LIVE life
with enjoyment -
I love myself.

When you pray,
I feel closer to God.

When you give to the world,
to others -
I seek God's purpose for me.

When you listen to me
and understand -
I know that God exists.

When you trust in God,
I know that everything is all good.

When you smile,
I know that all is right with the world.

So, please smile and be happy.

For when you are happy,
Everybody's Happy.

-Every Child

EVOLUTIONARY

Eons of answers to the question:
Where did we come from?

Your answer locates your culture

Trace the course of the storyline
Along the stones of people and place
That assuredly
Met your feet
As you crossed the river of meaning towards
The shore of your identity

This storyline is the cornerstone of your Reason

The cornerstone which holds you
In joy, in turbulence
In abundance and loss
In confusion and knowing
That which informs your body's
Outward expression

From which blueprint do you build Self?
What is your architecture?

How did you get here?

Do you come from the stars?
Are you born out of the underworld?
Are you made of a combining of chemicals?

Was your journey here a series of events?
A spiraling wave?
A gift? A punishment?
A miracle? A fluke?

Are you judged? Or loved?
To where do you return each day
And at the moment of your last breath?

Reach for the wisdom of your ancestors
Fold in your lived experience
Know what you wish for your descendants and

Create
Wildly, unabashedly, joyfully, prayerfully
Your story

Build
With the connections among your beautiful being
Your culture

Locate
Your cornerstone within your temple
And allow the world to touch you

BEFORE

Return to that awareness
which knows no favorites

Not foods, nor colors, peoples
What can be, in Oneness?

All are cherished
There is no here or there
this or that
wrong or right
bad or good

Before you were ever asked
to choose between two
or the many

Before you had to answer
which of these is not
like the other

Before you had to sort
which are the same
and which are the different

You knew Oneness
from the start
at the beginning

Return to this daily
for your centering.

This bliss, this balance
is your eternal home.

UNSPEAKABLE YOU

Unspeakable You
I feel your gaze
Behind my eyes

In the Void, All Eyes

My eyes bespeak confusion
Such is to think in the dark

Feel-see happens in heart-beat
In heart-sight
Darkness is breathing Light

You find me breathing
I find being

Behind my mind
I feel your gaze
Unspeakable You

ALLOWANCE OF BEING

Your insistence, my resistance,
Your persistence, my surrender
to His Will.

Fear of abandon
kept me from
submission, total
 liberation,

Giving up, giving in
seemed like loss of power.

As a leaf falls in total relaxation,
see its transformation
to dirt, then dust,
freed from weight
now carried by the same
empowering source.

Source not force.
Don't fear change.
Change is scary I know
Welcome imperative change

Find a workable model
until it works no more

Turn it upside down
which is right side up?

Search for meaning
not assignments

Allow, Allow, Allow
Keep listening…

RAINBOW BRIDGES

When was it a given that disintegration is necessary?
When will we reject being left behind?
When will we take all of us with us?
When will the center of our souls we find?

Remember you are a creator
Remember you are inviolate
Your powers rest in infinite patience
Until you reject being ruled by a surrogate

You are your own divine measure
Calibrated to intensities of light
You build bridges across chasms
When you step home to your worth, and unite

(chorus)
Stable, healed, integrated, full
Lively, vibrant, connected and whole
Expanded, voiced, seen, and loved
Complete, activated...all you dream of

There are never any mistakes
Every fall is another chance
Take it, open your eye wide inside
And say yes to another dance

For it is true we have each other
To help us remember our greatest gift
Deepening relationship with your deepest self
Allows the one immutable thing to come with

Open, open, open my dearest beloved
Unfold the closures and ignite your current
Stay impermeable yet mysteriously fluid
And nothing will be a deterrent

(chorus)
Stable, healed, integrated, full
Lively, vibrant, connected and whole
Expanded, voiced, seen, and loved
Complete, activated...all you dream of

I WONDER

It's the kind of day
of doing nothing
Yet something
Guides the way

The air thick with humidity
Like the rains, soon a'coming
Something is brewing, growing
Underground, inside, underneath

Doing nothing is still doing something
To do nothing and feel no guilt
No sense of urgency
No impending calamity

Just listening
Waiting to see
What wants to be born

Eyes half closed
This cloudy day
The storm now blown away

So close to sleep
Yet quite aware
Of the nothingness in all

So much work self-assigned
Which could be done
Now, not must or should or have to
Just could

In this present moment
Can I just be?
Reset to live in the now?

Release myself of the to-dos
Lists built for the future
In so many yesteryears

Today is that future –
It looks so little like the one
I planned or foresaw
Worked so hard for
Imagined in all those lists
Once I do this, then that

This is now, can I live
Day by day
In the here and now
In moment present
In alignment with Divine flow?

CURIOSITY

I wonder into myself
I wander what is in there…
This world, articulating joint
This word, genuflecting river…

My skin a July meadow
seeped in heat
I sit by the wild rose,
Close my eyes:
Unfurling petals
show me star codes

LOVE SHINE

When I was 6,
 He showed me
 with the wave of a human hand
 the Everywhere that was God

I saw the sunshine
 wind, and shimmering leaves,
 the trunk, the ground
 two sets of feet

With sudden awareness,
 it surged up through
 my body, the spark of
 the everywhere was in me!

I looked at once
 to the eyes belonging to
 the hands of She
 Who'd shown to me the Everywhere

Of which she knew
 but could not see
 that part of the Everywhere
 Was She!

With elation
 of truth of aliveness
 came that deep despair

Once awakened to
 The Great Truth

I wanted to only know next
For what
great purpose did you
born me?

The deep despair
formed questions too
What could cloud the eyes
of the heart and soul
who teaches children
of the presence of God?

Soon after I prayed to Him:
Please keep me innocent and pure

When one has found Spirit
and knows the truth of its existence
Ever-present, Every-where:
jubilation, exaltation, miracle of breath!
What can keep us from this essence?

Thus, the seeking began
to find why beauty
can get clouded over
and how to stay in
elation and joy

At 8,
Two years later
expelled from the country
of my birth.
joys in the adventure
sadness of the cruelty
of humanity

At 16,
My father left the house
4 children my mother to raise
on minimum wage
no more fights
She resolved her might
her sovereignty hard won
Now she felt a little less alone

At 16 too,
I fell in love
gave all my heart
hook line sinker dove
broken, shattered, torn apart
kept going back
he had said he was my soul mate

6 years later,
My heart mended
ready for another life
Met the man whom I would marry
He too, would break my heart
yet, I gave it all for the sake of fate

At 26,
I was learning how betrayal
could cloud the eyes of she
who turned inside
and kept the light alive
with enough intensity
to share with the child who was me
The child still inside who reminds
me to "Remember the light"
within, without, in the everything
and in the everywhere, that is He and She

At 36,
I birthed our child.
for this I had waited all my life
to be a mom, loving
like mine is to me
Euphoric and sleep deprived
blessed am I to raise this child
deeper is my commitment to family
Then this is the time
the husband decides
to look elsewhere for company
I felt like a nobody to him
And so, I became a Mom, even more

At 46,
Arrived the simple truths,
the answers I sought for so long
and along with came the remedy
He showed himself once more
reminding me the Him
to place above all others
To remember the light
To remember when I was six
in the everywhere and
in the somebody within
Who has a purpose
Who is a soul
Who has the spark
of life given
Miracle in flesh

At 56,
I share these joys
This light within
to shine it out
to remind others
of the beauty
We all share

This gift of grace
This spark of life
The inner light
for however short or long

Let's do that thing
We came to do
Look into my eyes
Reflect that light in you

And when your eyes are clouded
and someone shines their light on you
I hope you reflect a little back
because they need to see it, too.

Just keep loving…
    Just keep shining…
        Just keep smiling…

Smile - smile - smile
    Shine - shine - shine
        Love - love - love

JOURNEY INTO SELF

She stepped out onto the unobstructed plain. You could see the back of her head, lightening rod spine, sitting on the absorbent burnt sienna earth, her breath finally sifting down like nightfall, rolling off the cliffs and covering the ground fog-like and even. She sat. Closed eyes. Spread out her body into the distant landforms rising almost imperceptibly - blue only slightly more purple-grey than the dusk holding their outline soon to relinquish to starry night. And at some moment she walked forward smiling, hurting, thinking, emptying, wondering. She greeted the ground rising to her feet and beheld a flower, brilliant silk white, aroma of musk encircling her neck, jaw, eyes, crown, so fragrant, she leaned her head into its embracing smell, the smell of sun-baked skin. And each new step guided by yet another flower: a friendly yellow, an almost-translucent outline of rippled tulip-shape, a orchid of purple-comfort. And she found herself in clear thermal water. Pachamama's essence with a lotus unfurling by the dirt. Petal after petal unfurling as a sliver of moon-orb traipsed along the soft opening of night sky into Truth. "This is an opening," God said. And she stared naked into naked eyes of knowing. And poems became words. And she said, "Even let the scary flowers bloom." And he said: "Who decides to call them scary?" And she said, "I do." And he said: "They're simply all the other flowers." And they were a vast field of opening petals. Moving like a kelp forest. And Pachamama's snake unfurled from the base of her spine sitting on the bottom of the hot thermal waters and soft algae and krinkly pebbles and it spun and danced and sang and spiraled out of her head like a galaxy and all of the flowers were blooming and swaying and her insides, too, and she was not inhabiting a Name, escorted by expanding Grace. And breath created waves created an ocean lifting and lowering her in the swells. The tunnel of fire at the bottom of the sea floor had been traversed for the time being. And she remembered what is significant and she smiled and her breath rose with the swell again and continued on an upward thermal to meet the milky path. And she took another breath.

RETURN TRIP:
A LESSON ON THE LABYRINTH

Breath by breath,
Step by step

I'm walking back
out of the labyrinth

It doesn't look quite
the same

The things I
walked away from
on my path in,

I now face

The hurts and blame
The gifts of joy

Like wearing else's shoes
And seeing life reframed

So this is what it felt like
to be looking back at me

I hope you, too, now see
and we share
in equal empathy.

BEGINNINGS

A MIRACLE

I know this place of ecstasy -
better, maybe, than my own body;
outside of which it resides
and inclusive of it
at the same time.

Is it a specific place or was it a special time?

No!
I say it is within the eternal
and in the ever-present.

Glimpses, stretches and
States of mind,
Alignment of the stars,
Lightness of being.

These things I have felt
and seen with my own soul,
all that is possible where
once thought impossible,
is no longer considered a miracle.

And yet, still, very much, is.

MIRACLE

Windowed thoughts
Pose in the frame
Busy being
The Real Thing

Your breathing-heart self
Pays no mind
Currency is Free

The octopus has three hearts
And taste on every sucker

This is a miracle

MARKET CORRECTION

Oh, Money!
how we kneeled to you
a virus came
you buckle at your knees
a re-remind
who our true lord is:
Balance in all things

CURRENCY

Earth speaks a currency of abundance
Sun speaks a currency of vitality
Moon speaks a currency of nourishment
Stars speak a currency of infinitude
time to learn monetary languages
spoken by our ancestors

GOD'S GALLERY

Sometimes I feel
that God created
this beautiful masterpiece
called Earth
A finished piece
His body of work

Then like a gallery showing
He invited us humans
to have a viewing

We came, critiqued
chose certain art pieces
to take home

and God knows
what we did with them

Some forgot they were treasures
Some hung them up
to be admired,
Appreciated

Some tucked away
in some trunk
Well-preserved
or otherwise

Some used for other
than their intended purposes

So what was once a collection
is now dispersed
Rearranged
and God knows where

Sometimes I wonder
how we forgot
where we put the fragments
of ourselves

How we participated
in our own dismemberment
Thinking we were collectors
confused and astonished

God is eternally created
by the evolving creation

It is up to us
to teach ourselves
how to unpack our parts
Take them off display

Complete the body of work
as we complete ourselves
Becoming the mirrors through which
the Masterpiece can see itself, again

CREATING REALITY
WITH WORDS

In liminal space
Swirls of words
As changes hurl
Seeking center
New normal

Seeing open palette
Inspiring to create

Better world
Better way

Sorting existing threads
Self selecting

Weaving in
Fields of infinite
   possibility

Building new worlds
With words today

WHAT NOW?

Inside this vast vessel
You are self-sourced
Unlimited Free Energy:

unlocked through sacrament
    of compassionate heart
anointed in the naming
    of enlivened breath
understood through wisdom
    of focused awareness
nourished by action
    of aligned body

this is You,
all-ready
fully formed node
of re-generations

notice the current
you reside softly within
resonate the joy
of your relations,
sounding luminous stars

this will carry you home

the greatest service -
your becoming

NEW BEGINNINGS

We build with these words . . .

In the new world
True worth

Acknowledging
Wisdom teachings indigenous
Learned over millenniums

We live in gratitude
Of gifts by person,
City, state, nation
Country and by continent

Sharing caring
unity
accepting diversity
shining individuality
together in
Oneness

RADICLE - ODE TO 12/21/2020

The radicle has emerged!
...seed dropped from string of firmament plucked
By fingers of feeling
Absorbing quenching rains of focused intent...

Energy of a trillion suns.

And the rains poured en masse, and it was enough.

Down, down, grounding into the void
Defining Place
Now taking shape
Emerging from the dark
Opening into our lives,
Breathing us through its leaves of reality

May we tend and love this seedling
Every day, more leaves unfurl
in the lives of the people
Until there are enough stems
reaching into the perception of most

Then opens the dream flower
Of which we drink of our splendid gifts
Of life-giving creation

And a radical flourishing field of Love is our world!

BOOK MATTER

....

LANDING SPIRIT

Dear Reader,

You may wonder how the book you are reading came to be. You know that there is a story behind each one. And so it is with SPIRIT.

I have little memory of writing most of my poems. A secret pleasure where I allowed my creativity to freely express itself; full *poetic license*, as it were, setting aside any notions of how it is supposed to be done. It had become the practice of finding my voice. Many of the poems written due to an early promise to myself to "never" share them with anyone. *Never*, it turns out, is not forever, -just a holding - until you find a safe landing space.

Poems have spoken me awake since I can remember, connected me with my heart language, spoke truths I couldn't think into existence. Most of the poems I've ever written are lost to the scattering of life's rhythms; like dispersed leaves from endless years of fall breezes. Poetry has always been a solitary and non-possessive endeavor for me. There are only a few I have ever shared, mostly with family and close friends. I also began this Spirit journey with the idea that my poems were not something I would ever compile and bring out into the world.

Until…

Looking for connection one day on an upstart social media platform, I read one of Angela's poems. It spoke of nature, of divinity, the absolute ecstasy in meeting your creator, not all at once - rather in a subtle tender moment, and in perceiving the whole through this window. My poems were simple and light, yet, this is what most of them also attempted to express. Angela's poignancy resonated deeply within my core. They were my definition of poetry. Yes! This! I responded. More of this, please!!

A hand from an unexpected place laced her fingers within my poem's hand. A poem I tentatively shared on a start-up social media platform. Few people. Safe. A place to dip my toe. Saira's receptive hand felt warm, understanding, alive. A kindred spirit at first word. Connection.

Angela shared more poems, each one delighted me more than the one before. A desire to reciprocate emerged. Should I dare share mine with her? Would she even want to read them? Mine are a different "style" than hers, I sensed. I was an unfurling fern frond finding my way to the light. She was an upright branch fully rooted in her direction. Would she still appreciate them? I so wanted to share. Mustering up courage, I shared a couple of recently written ones.

And then she shared her poems in return.

I beheld endless worlds of complexity and great beauty held in all of their myriad intersecting truths, presented with simple, elegant, graceful lightness. Words for the everyday Heart of the People. Poems that we read and can understand and feel as real. Poems that hold the vastness of the human experience in terms we can touch. Yes! This! More of this!!

Saira's poems make sense of what my verbosity and self-perceived inaccessibility yearn for. Her rhythms are so natural and fun to move along with. Complimentary expressions, unique forms.

As I conveyed to Angela about the beauty of her poetry, the idea of exchanging more poetry came up. I panicked. I froze. Then, I released the idea of perfection. She said she was also not schooled in the subject like me. But hers *felt* like poetry to me. I wondered if my poetry could reach other's hearts, like Angela's had touched mine. What if she had never shared? After reading her poetry, the thought of having missed it, caused great heartache. Maybe I should share. Maybe someone would feel the same about my poetry.

It was the most natural thing in the world to share poems with Saira. Life-giving and inspiring. Safe. Welcomed. I didn't worry about "being a poet", because we honor each other's expression regardless of label, or technicality. The freedom to express so deeply, from such authentic places within, in a playful and joyful way lights me up. I have come to love a being I can trust with my softest places, and with whom I can reciprocate that service.

Angela accepted my poems unconditionally. Reflected them back to me. She gets them, I thought! An exchange of delight began. Expression meeting expression. Resonance meeting resonance.

Just like dancers twirling each other propelled into the next turn by the momentum of the previous one. Liberation through movement of Word.

After a time, Angela communicated an intention, and in it emerged the idea of a dance: a book of poetry combining our contrasting and complementary styles into a union. So our friendship and along with it, the idea grew of sharing it with others.

I so longed to experience the life-beyond-the-words of the poems we were sharing, and knew that together, they would create something wholly unique. Infused with joy, friendship, and acceptance, we could breathe new life into something previously so tenderly hidden and dormant to the world.

The Dance Begins.

I sent Angela a book of poems I compiled within our time together. She magically interwove a corresponding poem with each of mine. Wow, I thought, how did she do that? Did she just write them up quickly to match up so perfectly? Angela told me she had selected from her set of archived poems. I was more surprised and even more delighted. How could it be?

Each poem of Saira's was like a little being, that nestled upon my shoulder. I would read a poem, feel that being beside me, and find the poem of mine that was its friend. Sometimes I'd go right to it, and sometimes we'd amble a bit through my poems until the match was made. Friends! A total mirroring of our blossoming friendship as human beings...each poem a little door of discovery into a person I grew to love and admire.

I felt the uncloaking of the cocoon, letting go of the fears that had kept these poems in hidden pages. As a butterfly stretching its wings, I found opening my wings up to Angela was safe, joyful, fun! Sharing this passion with the world would be a good thing as well.

The Heart of the Dance

By now, we both cherished the friendship which had blossomed from the sharing of poetry. The saffron spot in the fabric of our friendship was when each of us read the other's poem to her. What a glorious honor to read another's words and to reflect back the inherent beauty of herself.

It was when we decided to edit the book and read the poems aloud to each other for sound, where the real heart of the poetry came alive for each of us. We read the other's poem to make sure they read as the writer intended. We were not so much editing at this stage as we were gauging for resonance and flow, energetic connection. An inexpressible expression of beauty unfolded. What happens after you put the poems on paper together? A process so intimate, so profoundly vulnerable emerged. Can you imagine what it's like to be held in unconditional love in your most vulnerable moment? Having my poems read to me, and the deep privilege of reading Saira's poems to her, was an act of incomprehensible empathy.

Then one day, Angela finished a poem of mine which had previously felt incomplete. Different sparks of delight! Another avenue of growth and resonance.

Another time, I wrote a poem reflecting one of hers. Once when re-reading through our gathered poems, I could not distinguish which one of us had written it. Was my memory playing tricks on me or was it uncovering another beautiful layer of the process?

This glorious being anointed with the gift of poignancy sharing her gifts, receiving mine - what an unfolding miracle in each moment to experience together. I see Angela. I hear Angela. I feel Angela's feelings. I feel seen, I feel heard. My feelings are felt. Reciprocity: the marvelous discovery of common threads and themes along the journey.

Dear Reader:

On these pages, you will find freedom of expression - poems of the heart, mind, spirit; insights from living this journey - ways in which Spirit reveals itself to us. It is a sharing from our souls to yours. We are grateful to you for reading our hearts. May you find resonance. May you feel heard. May you feel seen.

May you encounter us in these words and receive them with great love. May you see yourself reflected. May your heart be known and cherished through these words that affirm a great belonging to this world. Deepest of gratitude.

GRATITUDES

I send gratitude to Earth for sustaining all life. I send gratitude to Water for nourishing all life. I send gratitude to Air for enlivening all life. I send gratitude to Fire for transforming all life. I send gratitude to Center, for remembering all life. I send gratitude to my family and circle of loved ones for supporting my life. I send gratitude to Saira for seeing my life. I send gratitude to Self, for loving my life. I send gratitude to you, for reflecting life.

To You, Spirit, for the beauty of your creations.
To you, Mum, for the beauty of your creations.
To you, Angela, for the beauty of your creations.
I deeply thank you all.

Saira

Cherishing every moment on
Mother Earth.
I am in constant awe of the glory
of creation:
the beauty found in every flower,
the intricacy in every design,
the miracle of each
and every
existence.

Other Offerings from Saira:

Queen's Desire: a book poem

Floressence Cards: the soulful essence of flowers

Seek Joy, Find Beauty, Share Love, a photographic meditation

http://www.sairapriest.com

Angela

I wonder often about the infinite iterations of nature, I lay with trees, I am learning how to fully occupy myself. I want to stand wholly alongside Humanity, Plant, Animal, Fungus, Microbe, and Stone Nations. With elements, directions, astrals, stars, seeds, and compassionate spirits. I wander inner landscapes. I love love. I like listening to sounds and feeling vibrations massaging my cells. I am a reflection of you, the whole you. Thank you for reflecting the whole of me.

Join our poetry community:
www.spiritpoetrydance.com

Made in the USA
Columbia, SC
21 September 2022